CONTENTS

MIXED GREEN SALAD WITH
WARM CREAM CHEESE "CROUTONS"

PREP: 15 min. \ **TOTAL:** 15 min. \ **MAKES:** 8 servings, 1 cup each

---

4 oz. (½ of 8-oz. pkg.) *Philadelphia* Cream Cheese, cut into ½-inch cubes

¼ cup chopped *Planters* Sliced Almonds

8 cups torn salad greens

1 Granny Smith apple, thinly sliced

½ cup pomegranate seeds

⅓ cup *Kraft* Balsamic Vinaigrette Dressing

1 **Spray** large skillet with cooking spray; heat on medium heat. Meanwhile, coat cream cheese cubes with almonds.

2 **Add** cream cheese to skillet; cook 3 min. or until golden brown, turning occasionally.

3 **Combine** remaining ingredients in large bowl. Top with cheese. Serve immediately.

CREAMY LEMON-ASPARAGUS RISOTTO

PREP: 20 min. \ **TOTAL:** 20 min. \ **MAKES:** 6 servings

---

2 **Tbsp. olive oil**

1 **medium onion, finely chopped**

2 **cups instant white rice, uncooked**

½ **lb. fresh asparagus spears, cut into 1-inch lengths**

2 **cups chicken broth**

2 **Tbsp.** *Philadelphia* **Neufchâtel Cheese, softened**

Zest and juice from 1 lemon

1 **Heat** oil in large skillet on medium heat. Add onions; cook and stir 2 min. or until crisp-tender.

2 **Stir** in rice, asparagus and broth. Bring to boil. Reduce heat to low; simmer 5 min.

3 **Add** Neufchâtel, lemon zest and juice; cook until cream cheese is melted and mixture is well blended, stirring constantly.

SERVING SUGGESTION

Serve this risotto with grilled chicken or shrimp.

BUTTERNUT SQUASH PUFF

PREP: 10 min. \ **TOTAL:** 40 min. \ **MAKES:** 4 servings

- ¾ **cup dry bread crumbs, divided**
- 2 **cups mashed cooked butternut squash**
- 4 **oz. (½ of 8-oz. pkg.)** *Philadelphia* **Neufchâtel Cheese, softened**
- 2 **Tbsp. brown sugar**
- 1 **egg**

    Dash <u>each</u> **ground ginger, black pepper and salt**

1 **Heat** oven to 350°F.

2 **Reserve** ¼ cup bread crumbs. Mix remaining crumbs with remaining ingredients until blended.

3 **Spoon** into 1-qt. casserole sprayed with cooking spray; sprinkle with reserved bread crumbs.

4 **Bake** 30 min. or until heated through.

BACON & MAPLE SCALLOPED POTATOES

PREP: 25 min. \ **TOTAL:** 1 hour 30 min. \ **MAKES:** 8 servings, 1 cup each

- **1 red onion, thinly sliced**
- **4 oz. (½ of 8-oz. pkg.) *Philadelphia* Cream Cheese, cubed**
- **1 can (14½ oz.) fat-free reduced-sodium chicken broth**
- **½ cup milk**
- **¼ cup chopped *Oscar Mayer* Fully Cooked Bacon**
- **¼ cup maple-flavored or pancake syrup**
- **2 lb. Yukon Gold potatoes (about 8), cut into ¼-inch-thick slices**
- **1 cup *Kraft* Shredded Triple Cheddar Cheese with a *Touch of Philadelphia***

1 Heat oven to 400°F.

2 Cook onions in large skillet sprayed with cooking spray on medium-high heat 3 to 5 min. or until crisp-tender, stirring frequently. Remove onions from skillet.

3 Add cream cheese, broth and milk to skillet; cook and stir on medium-low heat 5 min. or until cream cheese is melted and mixture is well blended. Remove from heat; stir in bacon and syrup.

4 Place half the potatoes in 13×9-inch baking dish sprayed with cooking spray; cover with layers of onions and shredded cheese. Top with remaining potatoes and cream cheese sauce; cover.

5 Bake 1 hour 5 min. or until potatoes are tender and top is golden brown, uncovering after 50 min.

CREAMY VEGETABLE ORZO

PREP: 35 min. \ **TOTAL:** 35 min. \ **MAKES:** 6 servings, ½ cup each

---

- **1 Tbsp. oil**
- **1 small onion, chopped**
- **½ cup each chopped green and red peppers**
- **1 cup frozen corn**
- **¾ cup orzo pasta, uncooked**
- **1 can (14½ oz.) fat-free reduced-sodium chicken broth**
- **½ cup (½ of 8-oz. tub) *Philadelphia* Chive & Onion Reduced Fat Cream Cheese**

1 Heat oil in large skillet on medium heat. Add onions; cook 4 min., stirring frequently. Stir in peppers and corn; cook and stir 2 min. Add orzo; cook and stir 1 min.

2 Stir in broth; bring to boil on high heat. Simmer on medium-low heat 10 to 12 min. or until orzo and vegetables are tender and most of the liquid is absorbed, stirring occasionally.

3 Add cream cheese; cook 1 to 2 min. or until melted and sauce is well blended, stirring constantly.

SPECIAL EXTRA

Add 1 Tbsp. chopped fresh herbs, such as basil or rosemary, to the cooked vegetables with the broth.

ROASTED SWEET POTATO & CARROT PURÉE

PREP: 25 min. \ **TOTAL:** 1 hour 20 min. \ **MAKES:** 6 servings, ½ cup each

---

- **1 lb. sweet potatoes (about 2), peeled, cut into ½-inch pieces**
- **8 carrots (about 1 lb.), peeled, cut into ½-inch-thick slices**
- **3 Tbsp. olive oil**
- **2 Tbsp. brown sugar**
- **1 tsp. salt**
- **1½ cups chicken broth, divided**
- **4 oz. (½ of 8-oz. pkg.) *Philadelphia* Cream Cheese, cubed, softened**

1 Heat oven to 375°F.

2 Combine first 5 ingredients; spread onto bottom of 15×10×1-inch pan. Pour 1 cup broth over vegetable mixture.

3 Bake 45 to 55 min. or until broth is absorbed and vegetables are tender and caramelized, stirring occasionally.

4 Spoon vegetables into food processor. Add remaining broth and cream cheese; process until smooth. Return to pan; cook 10 min. or until heated through, stirring frequently.

SPECIAL EXTRA

Before processing roasted vegetables in food processor, reserve ½ cup of the vegetables to use as a garnish for the finished dish.

CREAMY CITRUS-CHIVE ASPARAGUS

PREP: 15 min. \ **TOTAL:** 15 min. \ **MAKES:** 6 servings

---

2 **lb. fresh asparagus spears, trimmed**

1 **Tbsp. water**

¼ **cup fat-free reduced-sodium chicken broth**

½ **cup (½ of 8-oz. tub)** *Philadelphia* **Chive & Onion Cream Cheese Spread**

½ **tsp. lemon zest**

1 **Place** asparagus in microwaveable casserole. Add water; cover with waxed paper. Microwave on HIGH 4 to 5 min. or until asparagus is crisp-tender.

2 **Meanwhile,** heat broth in small saucepan. Add cream cheese spread; cook until cream cheese is melted and sauce is slightly thickened, stirring constantly. Stir in zest.

3 **Drain** asparagus; top with sauce.

SERVING SUGGESTION

Divide cooked asparagus spears into 6 bundles and tie each with a steamed green onion for a simple and elegant presentation.

CREAMY DOUBLE-MASHED POTATOES

PREP: 15 min. \ **TOTAL:** 35 min. \ **MAKES:** 6 servings, ¾ cup each

---

 1 **lb. sweet potatoes (about 2), peeled, cut into chunks**

 1 **lb. red potatoes (about 3), peeled, cut into chunks**

 2 **oz. (¼ of 8-oz. pkg.) *Philadelphia* Neufchâtel Cheese, cubed**

 ½ **cup fat-free reduced-sodium chicken broth**

 4 **slices *Oscar Mayer* Bacon, cooked, crumbled**

1 **Cook** potatoes in boiling water in large saucepan 15 to 20 min. or until tender; drain. Return potatoes to pan.

2 **Add** Neufchâtel; mash potatoes just until blended. Gradually add broth, continuing to mash potatoes until of desired consistency.

3 **Stir** in bacon.

SUBSTITUTE
Substitute Yukon Gold potatoes for the red potatoes.

FABULOUS POTATOES

PREP: 20 min. \ **TOTAL:** 50 min. \ **MAKES:** 6 servings

---

  2 lb. baking potatoes (about 6), peeled, cubed

  1 pkg. (8 oz.) *Philadelphia* Cream Cheese, cubed

  1 cup *Breakstone's* or *Knudsen* Sour Cream

  2 green onions, chopped

1 Heat oven to 350°F.

2 Add potatoes to boiling water in saucepan; cook until tender. Drain.

3 Mash potatoes. Add cream cheese and sour cream; mash until fluffy. Spoon into greased 1-qt. casserole dish; cover.

4 Bake 30 min. or until heated through. Top with onions.

USE YOUR MICROWAVE

Mix all ingredients except onions as directed. Spoon into greased microwaveable 1-qt. casserole dish. Microwave on HIGH 8 to 10 min. or until heated through, stirring after 5 min. Top with onions.

CRUST-TOPPED BROCCOLI-CHEESE BAKE

PREP: 15 min. \ **TOTAL:** 45 min. \ **MAKES:** 14 servings

½ cup (½ of 8-oz. tub) *Philadelphia* Chive & Onion Cream Cheese Spread

1 can (10¾ oz.) condensed cream of mushroom soup

½ cup water

2 pkg. (16 oz. each) frozen broccoli florets, thawed, drained

1 cup *Kraft* Shredded Cheddar Cheese

1 frozen puff pastry sheet (½ of 17.3 oz. pkg.), thawed

1 egg, beaten

1 Heat oven to 400°F.

2 Mix cream cheese spread, soup and water in large bowl until blended. Stir in broccoli and Cheddar cheese. Spoon into 2½- to 3-qt. shallow rectangular or oval baking dish.

3 Roll pastry sheet on lightly floured surface to fit top of baking dish. Cover dish completely with pastry. Press pastry edges against rim of dish to seal. Brush with egg; pierce with knife to vent.

4 Bake 30 min. or until filling is heated through and pastry is puffed and golden brown.

TWICE-BAKED SWEET POTATOES

PREP: 20 min. \ **TOTAL:** 55 min. \ **MAKES:** 4 servings

- **2 large sweet potatoes (1½ lb.)**
- **2 oz. (¼ of 8-oz. pkg.) *Philadelphia* Neufchâtel Cheese, cubed**
- **2 Tbsp. fat-free milk**
- **1 Tbsp. brown sugar**
- **¼ tsp. ground cinnamon**
- **¼ cup chopped *Planters* Pecans**

1 Heat oven to 425°F.

2 Cut potatoes lengthwise in half; place, cut-sides down, in foil-lined 15×10×1-inch pan. Bake 30 to 35 min. or until tender.

3 Scoop out centers of potatoes into bowl, leaving ¼-inch-thick shells. Add Neufchâtel, milk, sugar and cinnamon to potato flesh; mash until blended.

4 Fill shells with potato mixture; top with nuts. Bake 8 min. or until potatoes are heated through and nuts are toasted.

EASY CARROT & BROCCOLI AU GRATIN

PREP: 25 min. \ **TOTAL:** 25 min. \ **MAKES:** 8 servings

---

  2 **cups baby carrots, cut in half**

  4 **cups small broccoli florets**

10 **round butter crackers, crushed**

  3 **Tbsp. *Kraft* Grated Parmesan Cheese**

  1 **Tbsp. butter, melted**

 ¼ **lb. *Velveeta*, cut into ½-inch cubes**

  2 **oz. (¼ of 8-oz. pkg.) *Philadelphia* Cream Cheese, cubed**

1 **Bring** 3 cups water to boil in large saucepan on medium-high heat. Add carrots. Reduce heat to medium-low; simmer 8 min. Add broccoli; simmer an additional 3 min. or until vegetables are crisp-tender. Meanwhile, mix cracker crumbs, Parmesan and butter until blended.

2 **Microwave** *Velveeta* and cream cheese in microwaveable measuring cup or medium bowl on HIGH 1 min.; stir. Microwave 30 sec. or until *Velveeta* and cream cheese are completely melted and mixture is well blended when stirred.

3 **Drain** vegetables; place in serving bowl. Top with cheese sauce; sprinkle with crumb mixture.

SHORTCUT

Look for ¾-lb. packages of fresh broccoli florets in the produce section of your supermarket. Each bag contains about 4 cups which is just the amount you need to prepare this tasty recipe.

CREAMED CORN

PREP: 10 min. \ **TOTAL:** 10 min. \ **MAKES:** 6 servings, ½ cup each

---

 2 oz. (¼ of 8-oz. pkg.) *Philadelphia* Cream Cheese, cubed

 2 Tbsp. milk

 3 cups frozen whole kernel corn, thawed

 1 can (14¾ oz.) cream-style corn

 ½ cup *Kraft* Shredded Cheddar Cheese

 ⅓ cup sliced green onions

1 Cook cream cheese and milk in medium saucepan on medium heat until cream cheese is melted, stirring frequently.

2 Add whole kernel corn and cream-style corn; stir. Cook 4 min. or until heated through, stirring occasionally.

3 Spoon into serving dish; sprinkle with Cheddar cheese and green onions.

SPECIAL EXTRA

If you like a hint of spice, stir in a dash or two of hot sauce.

EASY CAULIFLOWER & BROCCOLI AU GRATIN

PREP: 20 min. \ **TOTAL:** 20 min. \ **MAKES:** 10 servings, about ¾ cup each

- **5 cups large broccoli florets**
- **4 cups large cauliflower florets**
- **½ cup water**
- **4 oz. (½ of 8-oz. pkg.) *Philadelphia* Cream Cheese, softened**
- **¼ cup milk**
- **½ cup *Breakstone's* or *Knudsen* Sour Cream**
- **1½ cups *Kraft* Shredded Sharp Cheddar Cheese**
- **10 round butter crackers, crushed**
- **3 Tbsp. *Kraft* Grated Parmesan Cheese**

1 Place broccoli and cauliflower in 2-qt. microwaveable dish. Add water; cover. Microwave on HIGH 8 to 10 min. or until vegetables are tender; drain. Set aside.

2 Microwave cream cheese and milk in 2-cup microwaveable measuring cup or medium bowl 1 min. or until cream cheese is melted and mixture is well blended when stirred. Add sour cream; mix well. Pour over vegetables; sprinkle with Cheddar cheese. Microwave 2 min. or until cheese is melted.

3 Mix cracker crumbs and Parmesan cheese. Sprinkle over vegetables.

NOTE
For best results, cut the broccoli and cauliflower into similarly sized pieces before microwaving.